ISTANBUL: A TAPESTRY OF TIME

A Journey Through History, Culture, and Flavors.

LINDA H. BROWN

TABLE OF CONTENTS

Introduction To Istanbul

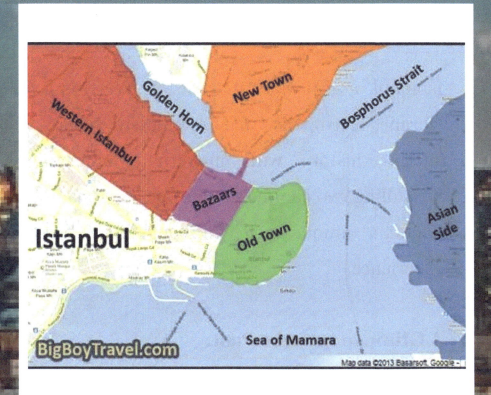

Istanbul: A Tapestry of Time and Tides

Istanbul, a city where East meets West, is a vibrant metropolis that seamlessly blends ancient history with modern dynamism. Straddling two continents, Europe and Asia, it offers a unique and unforgettable travel experience.

A Glimpse into the Past:

For centuries, Istanbul has been a crossroads of civilizations. Founded as Byzantium, it became the capital of the Roman Empire and later, the mighty Ottoman Empire. This rich history is woven into the fabric of the city, evident in its magnificent architecture, bustling bazaars, and diverse cultural tapestry.

A Symphony of Senses:

Prepare to be captivated by the city's sensory overload. The aroma of freshly brewed Turkish coffee mingles with the scent of spices at the Spice Market. The vibrant calls of street vendors echo through the Grand Bazaar, while the haunting melodies of the ezan (Call to prayer) drift from minarets that pierce the sky. The city pulsates with life, a constant symphony of sounds, sights, and smells.

A Mix of Old and New:

Istanbul is a city of contrasts. Ancient monuments like the Hagia Sophia and the Blue Mosque stand alongside modern skyscrapers. Traditional tea houses share the streets with trendy cafes, and bustling markets coexist with contemporary art galleries. This dynamic blend of old and new is what makes Istanbul so captivating and unique.

A City for Every Traveler:

Whether you're a history buff, a foodie, a shopaholic, or simply seeking an unforgettable adventure, Istanbul has something to offer. Explore the opulent palaces of the Ottoman sultans, wander through the labyrinthine streets of the Grand Bazaar, savor the flavors of Turkish cuisine, and soak in the vibrant atmosphere of this extraordinary city.

Get Ready to Be Enchanted:

Istanbul is more than just a destination; it's an experience. Prepare to be enchanted by its beauty, captivated by its history, and charmed by its vibrant spirit. This city will stay with you long after you've left, leaving an indelible mark on your soul.

Getting There & Around

Getting There & Around: Navigating Istanbul Like a Local

So, you're ready to embark on your Istanbul adventure! Whether you're arriving by plane, train, or even a ferry from a nearby island, the city offers a variety of ways to reach its heart. Let's explore the best options to get you settled in and ready to explore.

Flying In:
Istanbul is blessed with two major airports:

- **Istanbul Airport (IST):** The modern hub, located on the European side, is a major international gateway. It's well-connected with public transportation and offers a smooth arrival experience.

- **Atatürk Airport (ISL):** While gradually phasing out, it still handles some flights. If you're arriving here, expect a bit more hustle and bustle.

Once you've landed, here are your transportation options:

- **Public Transportation:** Istanbul boasts an efficient public transport system that's easy on the wallet. The metro, trams, and buses offer extensive coverage across the city. Purchase an Istanbulkart for seamless travel on all modes.

- **Taxis:** Yellow taxis are readily available, but be sure to use the meter or agree on a fare upfront. Ride-hailing apps like Uber and Yandex are also popular options.

- **Ferries:** The Bosphorus ferries are a must-try! They offer a scenic way to cross between the European and Asian sides, and you can even hop on a boat tour to explore the coastline.

Getting Around Like a Local:

- **Walk:** Istanbul is a city best explored on foot. Many neighborhoods are pedestrian-friendly, and you'll stumble upon hidden gems while wandering aimlessly.

- **Bike:** Rent a bicycle and explore the city at your own pace. Bike lanes are becoming more common, but be mindful of traffic.

- **Public Transportation:** Master the metro, trams, and buses, and you'll feel like a true Istanbullu. They're affordable, efficient, and offer a great way to experience the city's pulse.

Tips for a Smooth Journey:

- **Purchase an Istanbulkart:** This rechargeable card is your key to unlocking the public transport system. It's convenient, saves you money, and avoids the hassle of buying individual tickets.

- **Learn Basic Turkish Phrases:** While English is spoken in tourist areas, knowing a few basic phrases will enhance your interactions with locals.

- **Embrace the Journey:** Getting around Istanbul is part of the adventure. Don't be afraid to get lost in the labyrinthine streets or take a wrong turn. You never know what surprises await you.

Where to Stay:
Accommodation Options

Where to Stay: Finding Your Istanbul Nest

Choosing where to lay your head in Istanbul can be as exciting as exploring the city itself. From budget-friendly hostels to luxurious palaces transformed into hotels, there's something to suit every traveler's style and budget. Let's dive into the world of Istanbul accommodation and find your perfect nest.

For the Budget-Conscious Traveler:

- **Hostels:** Istanbul offers a vibrant hostel scene, perfect for solo travelers and those looking to meet fellow adventurers. Expect dorm rooms, private rooms, and social spaces where you can connect with other travelers.

- **Budget Hotels:** Many budget-friendly hotels are scattered across the city, often offering basic amenities like comfortable beds, private bathrooms, and Wi-Fi. Look for options in neighborhoods like Sultanahmet or Fatih for easy access to major attractions.

- **Guesthouses:** Charming guesthouses offer a more intimate and local experience. You might find yourself staying in a historic building or a cozy apartment, often with friendly hosts who can offer insider tips.

For the Mid-Range Traveler:

- **Boutique Hotels:** Istanbul is brimming with boutique hotels, each with its unique character and charm. Expect best decor, personalized service, and often, prime locations.

- **Apart-hotels:** These offer a home-away-from-home feel with kitchenettes, living areas, and laundry facilities. Perfect for families or those who prefer a bit more space and flexibility.

- **Traditional Ottoman Mansions:** For a truly unique experience, consider staying in a restored Ottoman mansion. These historic properties offer a glimpse into Istanbul's rich past, combined with modern amenities.

For the Luxury Traveler:

- **Palaces & Historic Hotels:** Indulge in the grandeur of Istanbul's past by staying in a former palace or a hotel housed in a historic building. Expect opulent decor, world-class service, and breathtaking views.

- **Boutique Hotels with Bosphorus Views:** Wake up to stunning views of the Bosphorus at one of Istanbul's many luxury hotels along the waterfront. Enjoy private balconies, rooftop terraces, and top-notch amenities.

- **Private Villas:** For a truly exclusive experience, rent a private villa in the outskirts of the city. Enjoy complete privacy, lush gardens, and breathtaking views.

Tips for Choosing Your Accommodation:

- **Consider your budget:** Set a realistic budget and explore options within your range.

- **Think about your travel style:** Do you prefer a social atmosphere, a quiet retreat, or something in between?

- **Choose a location that suits your interests:** If you want to be close to historical sites, Sultanahmet is a great choice. For a more local experience, consider neighborhoods like Balat or Karaköy.

- **Read reviews:** See what other travelers have to say about their experiences at different accommodations.

- **Book in advance:** Especially during peak season, it's advisable to book your accommodation well in advance to secure the best rates and availability.

Beyond the Room:

- **Look for unique features:** Many hotels offer special amenities like rooftop terraces, hammams, or even cooking classes.

- **Consider the neighborhood:** Choose a location that puts you within easy reach of the sights, sounds, and flavors of Istanbul.

- **Don't be afraid to negotiate:** Especially in smaller guesthouses and budget hotels, you might be able to negotiate a better price.

Finding the perfect place to stay is an important part of your Istanbul adventure. With a little research and planning, you'll find a nest that suits your needs and makes your stay in this incredible city even more memorable.

Must-See Attractions: Historical & Cultural Icons

Istanbul is a treasure trove of historical and cultural wonders, a living museum where every corner whispers tales of empires past. From awe-inspiring mosques to opulent palaces, the city beckons you to step back in time and immerse yourself in its rich heritage.

Hagia Sophia: Where Faith and History Converge:

No visit to Istanbul is complete without a pilgrimage to the Hagia Sophia. This masterpiece of Byzantine architecture has witnessed centuries of history, serving as a church, a mosque, and now, a museum. Its soaring dome, intricate mosaics, and awe-inspiring grandeur will leave you breathless.

The Blue Mosque: A Symphony in Blue:

Step into the serenity of the Sultanahmet Mosque, more commonly known as the Blue Mosque. Admire the breathtaking interior adorned with thousands of Iznik tiles, creating a mesmerizing symphony of blue. Don't forget to climb the minarets for panoramic views of the city.

Topkapi Palace: A Glimpse into Ottoman Grandeur:

Step into the opulent world of Ottoman sultans at Topkapi Palace. Explore the harem, admire the treasury filled with priceless jewels, and wander through the serene courtyards. This sprawling complex offers a fascinating glimpse into the grandeur and power of the Ottoman Empire.

Basilica Cistern: A Mysterious Underground World:

Venture beneath the city streets to discover the Basilica Cistern, a monumental underground water reservoir. Supported by a forest of towering columns, this eerie yet captivating space is a must-see for any visitor.

Grand Bazaar: A Sensory Overload:

Prepare for a sensory overload at the Grand Bazaar, a labyrinthine maze of shops overflowing with treasures. From carpets and ceramics to spices and Turkish delights, you'll find something to tempt every taste and budget. Don't forget to haggle and embrace the vibrant atmosphere!

Spice Market (Egyptian Bazaar): A Feast for the Senses:

Just a short walk from the Grand Bazaar, the Spice Market is a fragrant haven for spice lovers. Lose yourself in the intoxicating aromas of cinnamon, saffron, and countless other spices. Pick up some Turkish coffee, sample local delicacies, and soak in the vibrant atmosphere.

Beyond the Big Names: Hidden Treasures Await:

While the iconic attractions are a must, don't miss the opportunity to explore Istanbul's lesser-known gems. Wander through the serene courtyards of Süleymaniye Mosque, admire the intricate tilework at Rüstem Pasha Mosque, or explore the Chora Church with its stunning Byzantine mosaics.

Tips for Your Historical Exploration:

- **Plan Ahead:** Purchase tickets online in advance to avoid long queues, especially during peak season.

- **Dress Respectfully:** When visiting religious sites, dress modestly. Cover your shoulders and knees, and remove your shoes before entering mosques.

- **Hire a Guide:** Consider hiring a local guide to gain deeper insights into the history and culture of these iconic sites.

- **Take Your Time:** Don't rush your exploration. Allow yourself time to soak in the atmosphere, admire the details, and truly appreciate the grandeur of these historical wonders.

Exploring Neighborhoods:
Beyond the Tourist Trail

Istanbul isn't just about the iconic landmarks. To truly experience the city's soul, you need to venture beyond the well-trodden tourist paths and discover its vibrant neighborhoods. Each district has its own unique character, offering a glimpse into the everyday life of Istanbullus. Let's dive into a few of these captivating areas:

Sultanahmet: A Historical Heartbeat:
While undeniably touristy, Sultanahmet still holds a special charm. The grandeur of the Hagia Sophia and the Blue Mosque is undeniable. But beyond the crowds, explore the serene Gülhane Park, visit the Istanbul Archaeological Museums, or wander down the cobblestone streets, discovering hidden courtyards and antique shops. Don't miss the Hippodrome, a reminder of the city's ancient past.

Fatih: A Tapestry of Cultures:

Fatih is a melting pot of cultures, where Byzantine and Ottoman history intertwine. Explore the Grand Bazaar, a labyrinthine maze of shops selling everything imaginable. Immerse yourself in the vibrant atmosphere of the Spice Market, a riot of colors and aromas. Don't miss the Süleymaniye Mosque, a masterpiece of Ottoman architecture, and the serene courtyard of the Rustem Pasha Mosque.

Beyoğlu: The Heart of Modern Istanbul:

Beyoğlu is the beating heart of modern Istanbul. Explore the trendy boutiques and art galleries of İstiklal Caddesi, a lively pedestrian street. Take a ride on the historic Tünel funicular, offering stunning views of the city. Dive into the vibrant nightlife scene in the Taksim Square area, with its bars, clubs, and live music venues. Don't miss the charming French-inspired streets of Galata, with its antique shops and panoramic views from the Galata Tower.

Karaköy: A Creative Hub:

Karaköy is a trendy neighborhood with a bohemian vibe. Explore the art galleries, independent cafes, and trendy restaurants that line its cobblestone streets. Take a ferry across the Golden Horn to enjoy stunning views of the city skyline. Don't miss the vibrant art scene at SALT Galata, a contemporary art space housed in a historic bank building.

Balat: A Rainbow of Colors:

Balat is a charming neighborhood known for its colorful houses and multicultural history. Explore the narrow, winding streets, discovering hidden synagogues, churches, and historical buildings. Enjoy the relaxed atmosphere and the many cafes and art studios that have sprung up in recent years. Don't miss the Şemsipaşa Jewish Cemetery, a fascinating historical site.

Kadıköy: Asian Side Vibes:

Across the Bosphorus lies Kadıköy, a vibrant neighborhood with a distinct Asian side feel. Explore the bustling Kadıköy Market, a lively bazaar with a wide variety of goods. Enjoy the many cafes, bars, and restaurants that line the waterfront. Take a ferry to the nearby Princes' Islands for a peaceful escape from the city.

Tips for Exploring Neighborhoods:

- **Get Lost:** Wandering aimlessly is often the best way to discover hidden treasures and experience the true essence of a neighborhood.

- **Talk to Locals:** Strike up conversations with shopkeepers, resturant owners, and locals to get insider tips and recommendations.

- **Try Local Food:** Sample the flavors of each neighborhood by trying local specialties at small, family-run restaurants.

- **Embrace the Unexpected:** Be open to surprises and detours. The beauty of exploring neighborhoods is the unpredictability of the journey.

A Foodie's Paradise: Turkish Cuisine & Culinary Experiences

Turkish cuisine is a delicious tapestry of flavors and textures, influenced by centuries of history and cultural exchange. From street food stalls to Michelin-starred restaurants, Istanbul offers a culinary adventure for every palate.

A Taste of Turkish Classics:

- **Meze:** Start your culinary journey with a selection of meze, a collection of small dishes perfect for sharing. Think hummus, baba ghanoush, dolma (Stuffed grape leaves), and spicy çiğ köfte (Raw meatballs).

- **Kebabs:** No trip to Istanbul is complete without indulging in a kebab. From succulent döner kebap to juicy shish kebap, there are countless variations to satisfy every craving.

- **Mantı:** These delicate dumplings, filled with ground meat or cheese and topped with yogurt and garlic sauce, are a must-try.

- **Köfte:** From juicy meatballs to grilled kofta, this versatile dish comes in countless variations and is a staple of Turkish cuisine.

- **Baklava:** End your meal on a sweet note with baklava, a flaky pastry filled with nuts and drenched in honey.

Street Food Delights:

Istanbul is a street food paradise. Don't miss the chance to savor these iconic treats:

- **Simit:** A circular sesame-encrusted bread, perfect for a quick and tasty breakfast or snack.

- **Börek:** Flaky pastries filled with cheese, spinach, or potatoes, perfect for a savory bite.

- **Kokoreç:** Grilled lamb intestines, a unique and flavorful street food experience.

- **Midye Dolma:** Stuffed mussels, a simple yet delicious treat enjoyed by locals and tourists alike.

Beyond the Plate: Culinary Experiences

- **Turkish Coffee:** No visit to Istanbul is complete without sipping on a Turkish coffee, strong and flavorful, traditionally served in small cups.

- **Tea Culture:** Turkish tea is an integral part of daily life. Enjoy a steaming glass of çay at a local çay bahçesi (Tea garden) while watching the world go by.

- **Cooking Classes:** Learn the secrets of Turkish cuisine by taking a cooking class. You'll learn to prepare traditional dishes and gain valuable insights into the country's culinary heritage.

- **Food Tours:** Join a food tour to discover hidden Treaures and sample a variety of local delicacies.

Tips for a Foodie Adventure:

- **Explore Local Markets:** Visit the bustling Spice Market and Grand Bazaar to discover a world of spices, herbs, and local produce.

- **Dine Like a Local:** Venture beyond the tourist traps and explore the many small, family-run restaurants tucked away in the neighborhoods.

- **Embrace the Flavors:** Don't be afraid to step outside your comfort zone and try something new. You might be surprised by what you discover.

- **Savor the Experience:** Turkish cuisine is more than just food; it's a cultural experience. Take your time, savor each bite, and enjoy the journey.

Istanbul is a true foodie's paradise, offering a diverse and delicious culinary adventure. So, prepare your taste buds, embrace the flavors, and get ready to embark on a gastronomic journey through this captivating city!

Shopping Spree: From Grand Bazaar to Trendy Boutiques

Istanbul is a shopper's paradise! From the historic Grand Bazaar to trendy boutiques and hidden markets, the city offers a unique blend of traditional crafts, modern designs, and everything in between. Let's dive into the shopping scene and uncover some treasures.

The Grand Bazaar: A Labyrinth of Wonders:

No visit to Istanbul is complete without a trip to the Grand Bazaar. This sprawling marketplace, a labyrinth of covered streets and tiny shops, is a sensory overload. You'll find everything imaginable here: carpets, ceramics, jewelry, spices, leather goods, and more. Be prepared to bargain, it's expected and part of the experience.

Tips for the Grand Bazaar:

- **Go early:** Arrive early in the morning to avoid the midday heat and crowds.

- **Wear comfortable shoes:** You'll be doing a lot of walking!

- **Bargain wisely:** Start with a lower offer and be prepared to walk away if the price isn't right.

- **Don't be afraid to ask questions:** The shopkeepers are generally friendly and happy to answer your questions.

The Spice Market: A Feast for the Senses:
Just a short walk from the Grand Bazaar lies the Spice Market, a riot of colors and aromas. Here, mountains of spices, dried fruits, nuts, and Turkish delights tempt your senses. It's a feast for the eyes and the nose, and a great place to stock up on souvenirs and unique gifts.

Beyond the Bazaar:
Istanbul offers a diverse shopping scene beyond the traditional markets. Here are a few highlights:

- **Istiklal Caddesi:** This lively pedestrian street in Beyoğlu is lined with trendy boutiques, international brands, and independent shops.

- **Nişantaşı:** A chic neighborhood known for its high-end boutiques, designer stores, and upscale shopping centers.

- **Çukurcuma:** A charming neighborhood with antique shops, vintage stores, and art galleries.

- **Kadıköy:** Explore the bustling Kadıköy Market, where you'll find everything from local produce to handmade crafts.

Unique Shopping Experiences:
- **Support Local Artisans:** Look for shops selling handmade crafts, ceramics, and textiles made by local artisans.

- **Visit a Turkish Rug Shop:** Learn about the art of Turkish rug weaving and admire the intricate designs.

- **Take a Pottery Class:** Get hands-on and create your own souvenirs at a local pottery studio.

Tips for a Successful Shopping Spree:

- **Bargain respectfully:** Always be polite and respectful when bargaining.

- **Carry cash:** Many smaller shops and markets may not accept credit cards.

- **Check for quality:** Before you buy, carefully inspect the item for quality and craftsmanship.

- **Enjoy the experience:** Shopping in Istanbul is an adventure in itself. Embrace the hustle and bustle, and have fun!

Whether you're looking for authentic souvenirs, trendy fashion, or unique treasures, Istanbul has something for every shopper. So, put on your walking shoes, embrace the bargaining, and discover the city's vibrant shopping scene!

Bosphorus & Beyond: Boat Trips & Island Adventures

No trip to Istanbul is complete without experiencing the magic of the Bosphorus. This iconic waterway, separating Europe and Asia, offers breathtaking views, a glimpse into the city's maritime history, and a unique perspective on its sprawling landscape. Let's explore the best ways to enjoy this captivating waterway.

Bosphorus Cruises: A Must-Do Experience:

- **Public Ferries:** The most affordable and authentic way to experience the Bosphorus is by taking a public ferry. These ferries are a vital part of Istanbul's public transportation system, offering frequent crossings between the European and Asian sides. Enjoy the views, mingle with locals, and soak in the atmosphere.

- **Private Cruises:** For a more luxurious experience, consider a private cruise. You can choose from a variety of options, including dinner cruises, sunset cruises, and even romantic moonlight cruises. Many private cruises offer live music, delicious food, and drinks.

Island Hopping Adventures:

The Princes' Islands, a group of nine islands in the Sea of Marmara, offer a peaceful escape from the bustling city. These car-free islands are perfect for a day trip or a weekend getaway.

- **Büyükada:** The largest island, Büyükada, is known for its beautiful beaches, elegant mansions, and horse-drawn carriages. Rent a bike and explore the island's scenic roads, or simply relax on the beach and soak up the sun.

- **Heybeliada:** This island is home to monasteries, beautiful beaches, and lush forests. Hike to the top of the hill for stunning views of the surrounding islands.

- **Burgazada:** A smaller and quieter island, Burgazada is perfect for a relaxing getaway. Enjoy the charming cafes, art studios, and the island's laid-back atmosphere.

Tips for Your Bosphorus Adventure:

- **Choose the right time:** Sunset cruises offer breathtaking views, while morning cruises provide a more peaceful experience.

- **Dress comfortably:** Wear comfortable shoes, especially if you plan to explore the Princes' Islands.

- **Bring your camera:** Capture the stunning views of the city skyline, the Bosphorus, and the surrounding islands.

- **Embrace the local culture:** Chat with the ferry captains, enjoy Turkish tea on the deck, and soak in the vibrant atmosphere.

- **Respect the environment:** Avoid littering and be mindful of the impact of tourism on the delicate ecosystem.

Beyond the Bosphorus:

- **Golden Horn:** Explore the Golden Horn, a stunning inlet that winds its way through the heart of the city. Take a boat trip to see the colorful fishing boats and admire the historic waterfront.

- **Marmara Sea:** Embark on a day trip to the Marmara Sea, a vast body of water that separates Europe and Asia. Enjoy the stunning coastal scenery and explore the charming towns along the coast.

The Bosphorus is more than just a waterway; it's a symbol of Istanbul's unique identity and a gateway to unforgettable experiences. So, hop on a ferry, set sail, and discover the magic of this captivating city from a whole new perspective!

Nightlife & Entertainment: From Rooftop Bars to Live Music Venues

Istanbul comes alive after dark. The city's vibrant nightlife scene offers something for everyone, from rooftop bars with breathtaking views to traditional Turkish music performances and pulsating nightclubs. Let's explore some of the most exciting options:

Rooftop Bars: A View with a View:
Istanbul's rooftop bars are legendary. Perched high above the city, they offer stunning panoramic views, especially at sunset. Sip on a cocktail, enjoy the cool breeze, and soak in the magical atmosphere. Some popular rooftop bars include:

- **Mikla:** Located at the Marmara Pera Hotel, Mikla offers breathtaking views of the Bosphorus and the city skyline.

- **The Marmara Rooftop:** Another excellent option at the Marmara Pera Hotel, with a more relaxed and intimate ambiance.

- **Rixos Pera Istanbul:** This rooftop bar boasts a stunning infinity pool and offers a luxurious setting for enjoying the city views.

Live Music Venues: A Melodic Journey: Istanbul has a rich musical heritage, and the city's live music scene is thriving. From traditional Turkish music to jazz, rock, and electronic beats, there's something for every music lover. Check out these venues:

- **Nardis Jazz Club:** A legendary jazz club that has hosted some of the biggest names in jazz.

- **Babylon:** A popular live music venue that hosts a variety of acts, from Turkish rock bands to international DJs.

- **Dorock XL:** A large venue that hosts concerts by both local and international artists.

Traditional Turkish Music Performances:

Experience the soul of Istanbul by attending a traditional Turkish music performance. You can find these performances at:

- **Hodjapasha Cultural Center:** A historic building that hosts regular performances of traditional Turkish music and dance.

- **Semazen Show:** Witness the mystical whirling dervishes perform their mesmerizing ritual at the Hodjapasha Cultural Center or other designated locations.

Nightclubs: Dance the Night Away:

If you're looking to dance the night away, Istanbul has a vibrant club scene. Check out these popular clubs:

- **Reina:** A legendary nightclub located on the Bosphorus, known for its glamorous atmosphere and international DJs.

- **Babylon Bosphorus:** An outdoor club with stunning views of the Bosphorus, perfect for summer nights.

- **Sortie:** A trendy nightclub in the Beyoğlu district, popular with a younger crowd.

Tips for Experiencing Istanbul's Nightlife:

- **Dress appropriately:** While Istanbul is a relatively casual city, dress codes can vary at some upscale bars and clubs.

- **Arrive early:** Popular venues can get crowded, so arrive early to avoid long queues.

- **Try local drinks:** Sample some traditional Turkish drinks like raki (Anise-flavored liquor) or Turkish beer.

- **Be respectful of local customs:** Be mindful of noise levels and avoid disturbing the neighborhood.

Istanbul's nightlife is a vibrant tapestry of sounds, sights, and experiences. Whether you're looking for a romantic rooftop bar, a lively music venue, or a pulsating nightclub, the city has something to offer. So, embrace the night, explore the city's vibrant nightlife scene, and create unforgettable memories.

Day Trips & Excursions: Exploring Beyond the City

Istanbul is a vibrant metropolis, but its magic extends far beyond the city limits. The surrounding region offers a wealth of day trip and excursion opportunities, from historical sites and natural wonders to charming towns and hidden treasures. Let's explore some of the most captivating destinations within easy reach.

Historical Sites:

- **Ephesus:** Journey back in time to the ancient Greek city of Ephesus, a UNESCO World Heritage Site. Explore the well-preserved ruins of the Temple of Artemis, the Library of Celsus, and the Great Theatre.

- **Troy:** Discover the legendary city of Troy, immortalized in Homer's epic poem, the Iliad. Explore the archaeological site and learn about the fascinating history of this ancient city-state.

- **Hierapolis & Pamukkale:** Witness the breathtaking travertine terraces of Pamukkale, a natural wonder formed by mineral-rich hot springs. Explore the ancient ruins of Hierapolis, a UNESCO World Heritage Site, located nearby.

Natural Wonders:
- **Princes' Islands:** Escape the city bustle with a ferry ride to the Princes' Islands, a group of nine islands in the Sea of Marmara. Enjoy the car-free environment, relax on the beaches, and explore the charming villages.

- **Bosphorus Cruise:** Embark on a scenic cruise along the Bosphorus Strait, admiring the city skyline, opulent palaces, and charming waterfront neighborhoods.

- **Black Sea Coast:** Take a day trip to the Black Sea coast, known for its stunning natural beauty, lush forests, and charming coastal towns.

Charming Towns:

- **Çatalca:** Escape the city and explore the peaceful countryside of Çatalca, known for its vineyards and olive groves. Enjoy a wine tasting at a local winery or simply relax in the tranquil atmosphere.

- **Sile:** Discover the charming seaside town of Sile, with its picturesque harbor, sandy beaches, and historical lighthouse. Enjoy a seafood feast at a waterfront restaurant and soak in the laid-back atmosphere.

Tips for Day Trips and Excursions:

- **Plan Ahead:** Book tickets and tours in advance, especially during peak season.

- **Choose Comfortable Transportation:** Consider joining a guided tour with transportation included or renting a car for more flexibility.

- **Pack Essentials:** Don't forget to pack sunscreen, a hat, and comfortable walking shoes.

- **Respect Local Customs:** Dress modestly when visiting religious sites and be mindful of local traditions.

- **Embrace the Unexpected:** Be open to spontaneous detours and unexpected discoveries.

Beyond the City Limits:
Istanbul is a gateway to a wealth of historical and natural wonders. By venturing beyond the city, you'll gain a deeper understanding of Turkish culture and history, and experience the diverse landscapes and charming towns that make this region so special.

Culture and Arts: Museums, Galleries, and Performances

Istanbul is a vibrant cultural hub, where history, art, and tradition come alive. From world-renowned museums to hidden galleries and captivating performances, the city offers a feast for the senses. Let's explore the rich tapestry of culture that Istanbul has to offer.

Museums: A Journey Through Time:
Istanbul boasts a wealth of museums that showcase the city's rich history and cultural heritage.

- **Istanbul Archaeological Museums:** This sprawling complex houses a vast collection of artifacts from ancient civilizations, including Roman, Byzantine, and Ottoman empires.

- **Hagia Sophia Museum:** This iconic Byzantine basilica, now a museum, is a marvel of design and a testament to Istanbul's rich history. Explore its intricate mosaics, soaring domes, and awe-inspiring architecture.

- **Topkapi Palace Museum:** Step back in time at this opulent palace, once home to Ottoman sultans. Explore the harem, the treasury, and the magnificent courtyards.

- **Chora Church Museum:** Admire the breathtaking Byzantine mosaics and frescoes that adorn the walls of this historic church.

Art Galleries: A Modern Expression:
Istanbul is experiencing a contemporary art renaissance, with numerous galleries showcasing the work of local and international artists.

- **İstiklal Caddesi:** This vibrant street is home to many art galleries, showcasing a range of contemporary art styles.

- **SALT Galata:** This contemporary art space, housed in a historic bank building, features thought-provoking exhibitions and events.

- **Contemporary Istanbul:** This annual art fair is a major event on the international art scene, showcasing the work of leading contemporary artists.

Performances: A Cultural Celebration:
Istanbul's cultural scene is alive with music, dance, and theater performances.

- **Turkish Classical Music Concerts:** Experience the haunting melodies of Turkish classical music at a traditional concert.

- **Whirling Dervishes Ceremony:** Witness the mesmerizing ritual of the whirling dervishes, a Sufi practice that dates back centuries.

- **Theater Performances:** Catch a play or a musical at one of Istanbul's many theaters.

- **Traditional Puppet Shows:** Enjoy a traditional Turkish puppet show, a captivating form of storytelling.

Tips for Exploring the Cultural Scene:

- **Check for special events:** Many museums and galleries host special exhibitions and events throughout the year.

- **Consider a museum pass:** If you plan to visit multiple museums, consider purchasing a museum pass for discounted entry.

- **Book tickets in advance:** For popular performances and exhibitions, it's advisable to book tickets in advance to avoid disappointment.

- **Embrace the local scene:** Don't be afraid to venture off the beaten path and explore smaller galleries and local performances.

Wellness and Relaxation: Spas, Hammams, and Green Spaces

Wellness and Relaxation: Spas, Hammams, and Green Spaces

Istanbul is a city that invites you to slow down and savor the moment. Amidst the hustle and bustle, you'll find oases of tranquility where you can rejuvenate your mind and body. From traditional Turkish baths to serene green spaces, there are plenty of opportunities to unwind and recharge.

A Hammam Experience: A Turkish Tradition:

No visit to Istanbul is complete without a traditional Turkish bath experience. Hammams are more than just places to clean; they are social spaces where people have gathered for centuries to relax, socialize, and rejuvenate.

- **The Ritual:** A typical hammam experience involves a series of steps, including a hot steam room, a vigorous scrub, and a relaxing foam massage.

- **Where to Go:** Cemberlitas Hamam and Çukurcuma Hamam are popular choices, offering a classic hammam experience.

- **Tips:** Go with a friend or partner for a more social experience. Wear comfortable clothing and bring your own towel.

Spas and Wellness Retreats:
Istanbul offers a range of modern spas and wellness centers where you can indulge in a variety of treatments.

- **Massage:** Enjoy a traditional Turkish massage, aromatherapy, or a deep tissue massage to relieve tension and stress.

- **Facials:** Pamper your skin with a luxurious facial using natural products.

- **Wellness Retreats:** Several retreats offer yoga classes, meditation sessions, and healthy dining options for a holistic wellness experience.

Green Spaces for Relaxation:

Escape the city bustle and find tranquility in Istanbul's many green spaces.

- **Gülhane Park:** Located next to the Topkapi Palace, this serene park offers a peaceful escape from the crowds.

- **Emirgan Park:** Known for its stunning tulip gardens, Emirgan Park is a beautiful place to stroll and enjoy the natural beauty.

- **Yıldız Park:** This sprawling park offers breathtaking views of the Bosphorus and is a popular spot for picnics and leisurely walks.

Tips for Relaxation in Istanbul:

- **Start your day with a Turkish breakfast:** Enjoy a leisurely breakfast at a local cafe and soak in the morning atmosphere.

- **Take a break from sightseeing:** Schedule some downtime in your itinerary to relax and recharge.

- **Embrace the slow pace of life:** Take your time, savor the moment, and enjoy the Turkish way of life.

- **Indulge in a Turkish tea:** Enjoy a cup of strong Turkish tea at a local tea garden and watch the world go by.

Istanbul offers a unique mix of ancient traditions and modern wellness practices. Whether you're seeking a traditional hammam experience, a luxurious spa treatment, or simply a peaceful escape in nature, you'll find plenty of opportunities to relax and rejuvenate in this vibrant city.

Travel Tips for Women: Safety, Respect, & Empowerment

Traveling as a woman can be an incredibly enriching experience, opening doors to new cultures and adventures. However, it's important to be mindful of your safety and navigate cultural nuances. Here are some tips to help you have a safe, respectful, and empowering travel experience in Istanbul:

Safety First:

- Research and Plan: Before you travel, do your research on the neighborhoods you plan to visit, transportation options, and any potential safety concerns.

- Trust Your Instincts: If something feels off, don't hesitate to change your plans or leave a situation. Your safety is paramount.

- Dress Comfortably and Respectfully: While Istanbul is a modern city, it's important to be mindful of cultural norms. Dress modestly, especially when visiting religious sites.

- Stay Connected: Let someone know your itinerary and check in with them regularly. Consider using a travel safety app that allows you to share your location with loved ones.

- **Be Aware of Your Surroundings:** Pay attention to your surroundings and avoid walking alone at night in deserted areas.

Respecting Local Customs:
- **Dress Modestly:** When visiting religious sites, cover your shoulders and knees.

- **Learn Basic Turkish Phrases:** Even a few basic phrases can go a long way in showing respect and building rapport with locals.

- **Avoid Public Displays of Affection:** Public displays of affection may not be considered appropriate in all situations.

- **Be Mindful of Body Language:** Maintain eye contact and a firm handshake when greeting people.

- **Respect Local Traditions:** Take the time to learn about and respect local customs and traditions.

Empowering Yourself:

- **Travel Confidently:** Projecting confidence can help deter unwanted attention.

- **Learn Basic Self-Defense:** Consider taking a self-defense class before your trip.

- **Connect with Other Women Travelers:** Join online travel groups or forums for women to connect with other travelers and share experiences.

- **Support Women-Owned Businesses:** Look for opportunities to support women-owned businesses, such as cafes, shops, and tours.

- **Embrace the Experience:** Traveling as a woman can be an empowering experience. Embrace the challenges, celebrate your independence, and enjoy the adventure!

Resources for Women Travelers:

- **Travel blogs and forums:** Many travel blogs and forums cater specifically to women travelers, offering valuable advice and safety tips.

- **Local women's organizations:** Research local women's organizations in Istanbul for support and resources.

- **Embassies and consulates:** Contact your embassy or consulate in Istanbul for any safety concerns or emergencies.

Remember: These are just a few general tips. Every traveler is different, and it's important to adapt these tips to your own travel style and comfort level. By being aware of your surroundings, respecting local customs, and taking proactive steps to ensure your safety, you can have an unforgettable and empowering travel experience in Istanbul.

Sustainable Travel: Eco-Friendly Practices & Responsible Tourism

Sustainable Travel: Eco-Friendly Practices & Responsible Tourism

As travelers, we have a responsibility to minimize our impact on the environment and support the local communities we visit. Sustainable travel is more than just a buzzword; it's about making conscious choices that protect our planet and enrich the lives of the people we encounter.

Eco-Friendly Practices:
- **Choose Eco-Friendly Accommodation:** Look for hotels and guesthouses with sustainable practices, such as using renewable energy, reducing water consumption, and minimizing waste.

- **Embrace Public Transportation:** Conclude for public transportation like the metro, trams, and buses whenever possible. Walking and cycling are also excellent ways to explore the city.

- **Minimize Waste:** Carry a reusable water bottle and avoid single-use plastics. Bring your own bags for shopping and choose reusable utensils and containers.

- **Conserve Water and Energy:** Turn off lights and appliances when not in use, and take shorter showers.

- **Respect Nature:** Avoid littering and stay on designated trails when hiking or exploring natural areas.

Responsible Tourism:

- **Support Local Businesses:** Choose to eat at locally-owned restaurants, shop at small boutiques, and book tours with local operators.

- **Respect Local Customs and Traditions:** Dress modestly when visiting religious sites, learn a few basic Turkish phrases, and avoid loud or disruptive behavior.

- **Bargain Ethically:** While bargaining is expected in some markets, be mindful of the impact on local livelihoods. Don't haggle excessively, especially with small vendors.

- **Learn About Local History and Culture:** Take the time to learn about the history, culture, and traditions of the places you visit. Attend cultural performances, visit museums, and engage with local communities.

- **Give Back to the Community:** Consider volunteering your time at a local organization or making a donation to a worthy cause.

Organizations Promoting Sustainable Tourism in Istanbul:

- **Slow Tourism Istanbul:** This organization promotes sustainable and responsible travel practices in the city, offering walking tours, cycling tours, and cultural experiences.

- **Green Istanbul:** This platform provides information on eco-friendly businesses, sustainable tourism initiatives, and environmental awareness campaigns.

Tips for Sustainable Travel in Istanbul:

- **Visit during the shoulder seasons:** Traveling during the spring or fall can help avoid peak crowds and reduce your impact on the environment.

- **Choose experiences that support local communities:** Consider taking a cooking class, attending a traditional Turkish music performance, or participating in a community-based project.

- **Travel mindfully:** Be aware of your environmental impact and make conscious choices throughout your trip.

Sustainable travel is not about sacrificing your enjoyment; it's about making conscious choices that enrich your travel experience while minimizing your impact on the environment and supporting the local community. By embracing these principles, you can travel responsibly and leave a positive mark on the world.

Appendix: Useful Information and Resources

Appendix: Useful Information & Resources:

So, you're ready to embark on your Istanbul adventure! This appendix is your go-to guide for essential information and resources to help you navigate the city and make the most of your trip.

Currency:

- The official currency of Turkey is the Turkish Lira (TRY).

- ATMs are readily available throughout the city.

- Credit cards are widely accepted in major hotels, restaurants, and shops, but cash is often preferred in smaller establishments and markets.

- It's always a good idea to carry some cash for tips, transportation, and smaller purchases.

Language:

- The official language of Turkey is Turkish.

- While English is spoken in tourist areas, learning a few basic Turkish phrases will enhance your interactions with locals.

- Consider downloading a translation app to help you communicate.

Communication:

- **Phone:** Purchase a local SIM card for affordable international calls and mobile data.

- **Wi-Fi:** Free Wi-Fi is available in many cafes, restaurants, and hotels.

Transportation:

- **Istanbulkart:** This rechargeable card is essential for using public transportation (Metro, trams, buses, ferries). Purchase it at metro stations or kiosks.

- **Taxis:** Yellow taxis are readily available, but be sure to use the meter or agree on a fare upfront. Ride-hailing apps like Uber and Yandex are also popular options.

- **Ferries:** The Bosphorus ferries are a must-try! They offer a scenic way to cross between the European and Asian sides.

Emergencies:

- Emergency Numbers: Police: 155
- Ambulance: 112
- Fire: 110

- **Embassy/Consulate:** Contact your country's embassy or consulate in Istanbul for any emergencies or assistance.

Useful Resources:

- **Istanbul Tourist Information Office:** Provides information on attractions, events, and travel tips.

- **Google Maps:** An invaluable tool for navigating the city, finding attractions, and locating nearby restaurants and shops.

- **TripAdvisor:** Read reviews and compare prices for hotels, restaurants, and tours.

- **Istanbulkart website:** For information on purchasing and using the Istanbulkart.

Additional Tips:

- **Dress comfortably:** Wear comfortable shoes as you'll be doing a lot of walking.

- **Stay hydrated:** The weather in Istanbul can be hot, especially during the summer months. Carry a water bottle and stay hydrated.

- **Respect local customs:** Dress modestly when visiting religious sites and be mindful of local traditions.

- **Bargain respectfully:** Bargaining is expected in many markets and shops.

- **Enjoy the journey!** Istanbul is a vibrant and exciting city. Embrace the unexpected and enjoy the adventure.